GET IN THE RING

The Tale of Bruno the Boxer

A fable about living your dreams.

Stephanie Himango

GET IN THE RING
The Tale of Bruno the Boxer

ISBN-13: 978-1546360278
ISBN-10: 1546360271

Los Angeles, California 2017

Contents

This book is dedicated...
To those who seek
To those who struggle
To those who fall
To those who stand up again
To those who dare
To those who lend a hand
To those who serve
To those who encourage
To those who uplift
To those who trust
To those who box
To those who believe
To those who love
To those who get in the ring.

Introduction

"I don't want to be better than you or her or him.
I want to be better than I am right now."
Kerri Walsh Jennings

This is a story about a boy. But it could just as well be a story about a girl. The themes that are subtly incorporated into this fable are universally applicable for females, males, adults and teens. We all share the human experience.

I hope this story will inspire thought and discussion on important subjects including love, fear, grace, mentorship, thought patterns, judgment, limiting beliefs, kindness, mindfulness, encouragement, determination, courage, inner conflict, self-doubt, self-love, respect, humility, service, caring, patience, spirituality, insight, perseverance, openness, resilience, possibility and reaching our highest potential.

My dream is this story will leave you with hope and inspiration to get in the ring of your choice. What is your ring? Speaking up? Reclaiming your health? A diploma? A hard conversation? Living your truth? Addressing addiction? Growth happens when we participate in life, despite the critics. Change happens when we walk on uncertain ground and through uncertain times. Life happens when we get in the ring.

May you find the courage to get in the ring of your life.

Chapter 1

The Dream

*"The future belongs to those
who believe in the
beauty of their dreams."*
Eleanor Roosevelt

Bruno the boxer puppy loved the boxing gym. The smell of it, the sound of it, everything. His floppy ears and big paws made him look sweet, but like most boxers, his little face was already handsome and serious. His eyes were beautiful pools of black. He was in his happy place, but his heart was heavy.

I want to be a boxer, he thought. *I'm just a puppy, but I want to be a real boxer.* He could feel this desire with all his heart. He'd never wanted something so much in the world.

The trainers and people boxers at the gym always smiled so big when they saw him. Sometimes they rubbed his head or shook him by one of his white socked paws. Some people talked to him. And the really open-hearted people looked in his eyes and asked him how he was doing. They even seemed to wait for his answer. His favorite boxing trainer, Pops, always did this.

"Hi Bruno. How are you today?" Pops said, gently scratching behind Bruno's ears. "What are you thinking about? Hm? What are you thinking about?" Pops gave him a good rub on his head and chuckled.

Pops is a world-class boxing trainer and has been in the game a long time. Strong, smart and a talented technician, Pops takes his role beyond trainer, to teacher. He is respected by friends and strangers who know his work and personality — always a mix of humility and class — and when appropriate, silliness and a colorful vocabulary. He treats his fighters like sons. He doesn't try to make them something they're not. He helps them become the very best version of themselves. He believes in them. Even though Bruno knew he was just a little boxer puppy, he loved that Pops made him feel like a champ.

All those times when people asked Bruno what he was thinking, he wanted to answer. But since he couldn't talk like people do, he tried his best to communicate with his eyes.

If he could speak, he would have told them he wished he was big enough to reach the speed bag and especially the boxing ring. He would have told them he watched them spar. He would have told them he could see their courage. He would have told them he knew when they were scared. He would have told them he could see their heart. He would have told them how much he admired them. Most of all, if Bruno could talk, he would have told them he wanted to be like them. Not just a boxer puppy. A boxer.

Morning light sliced through the gym windows, and to Bruno it felt like summer again. He dropped his little nose into the bowl with a B on it and drank up the last of his water. He looked up at the people, walking ankle high to the tallest ones, then circled his tail and plopped into a curled ball along a warm strip of sun. He stretched his neck and rested his chin on the floor as his eyes scanned the room.

I want to be a boxer. His eyes closed for a second, then he tried to open them again.

To the rhythm of the speed bag, he drifted off to sleep. Before he knew it, the speed bag sounds were louder and faster, and he was being swept through a tunnel of sparkling light and ear-moving sound … all crescendoing into a gleaming dreamy amplified version of this very same room!

Chapter 2

The Light

"Inaction breeds doubt and fear.
Action breeds confidence and courage.
If you want to conquer fear, do not sit home and think about it.
Go out and get busy."
Dale Carnegie

The light became intense, and then *poof!* Bruno was across the room and standing on a low wooden platform used for jumping rope. Wow! He'd been here so many times before but usually just sniffing around and slipping across the floor.

Gold and white specks of light floated all around him, and when they fell away, an incredible vision was revealed in the mirror. He was transformed! Bruno was a small-framed 18 year-old boy! What happened? He was still wearing tall white socks just like he had when he was a puppy, but he was a boy now, and this boy was shadow boxing!

His skin tingled and a few more glints of gold glimmered from his arms and legs. A faint mist of white light danced from his socks. As the sun began shining on the side of his face, he moved: practicing punches, defensive moves and footwork. *Am I dreaming?* thought Bruno. *Being a boy and boxing is a dream come true!*

Behind him, inviting like a glassy swimming pool, he could see the elevated boxing ring. It was empty. Perfectly still, the ropes stretched around its perimeter like quiet guards. That was where Bruno wanted to be. He wanted to feel his feet on the smooth stretch of canvas, and he imagined the thrill of moving in that space. But

Bruno's mind told him the boxing ring was for bigger and better boxers. He feared what other people would think. He feared being judged. He feared rejection. So Bruno stayed down, near the corner, where he felt safe. In that moment, his puppy body vanished completely and his human essence crystallized. And like an uninvited guest to his human form, self-doubt had already started to make its insidious move.

Bruno had studied boxing for a long time, so he could see in the mirror what he was doing well and what needed practice. He stayed light on his feet and concentrated on his footwork and his jab. But his focus had already begun to falter. One part of his mind was fighting to take a risk and follow a dream. The other part was fighting to stay safe and invisible. Bruno knew he belonged at the gym, but he couldn't bring himself to do something as basic as get up in the ring and shadow box. For some reason, it terrified him to the extent that it didn't really even make sense.

"Get in the ring," said someone approaching Bruno from the side. Bruno pivoted and saw that it was Pops, smiling and carrying his gym bag and hot tea.

"Morning!" Bruno managed to say through his labored breath.

"Good morning," said Pops, still grinning. "Why are you shadow boxing down here? Get in the ring."

Bruno smiled a little to show respect and continued shadow boxing. He was scared to get up in the ring. Pops could see that, so he stopped and looked at Bruno a little harder. Eyebrows raised, and with a hint of a smile, Pops said again in a slow encouraging tone: "Get in the ring." Now Bruno was smiling too. "Get in the ring. Move around," Pops persisted.

Even though he was young, somewhere inside, Bruno knew he was living small. He wanted to be brave. But he wasn't even in the ring! Bruno's Dad had told him that boxing was like life. And from what Bruno could see, he was living on the outskirts of life just like he was on the outskirts of the ring.

Bruno missed his Dad. His Dad knew about getting in the ring. He had been a boxer. And when Bruno was little, the two of them would lay down on the floor and look through his Dad's photo albums. His Dad would stir Bruno's imagination, pointing to the pictures and telling boxing stories. His Dad told him boxing was about developing a strong mind. He said boxing was about having courage and taking risks. He said boxing was about trusting your instincts. He said boxing was about avoiding hits, but absorbing the ones that got through and learning from them. He said boxing was about not giving up. He said boxing was about training hard in private, then getting in the ring and being seen.

How could Bruno's dream of becoming a real boxer come true if he didn't even get in the ring? Inside his pocket, Bruno felt the piece of paper his Mom had given him. He had read the message so many times that he had the powerful words memorized. But every day, he needed the reminder.

The Man In The Arena
"It is not the critic who counts; not the man who points out how the strong man stumbles, or where the doer of deeds could have done them better. The credit belongs to the man who is actually in the arena, whose face is marred by dust and sweat and blood; who strives valiantly; who errs, who comes short again and again, because there is no effort without error and shortcoming; but who does actually strive to do the deeds; who knows great enthusiasms, the great devotions; who spends himself in a worthy cause; who at the best knows in the end the triumph of high achievement, and who at the worst, if he fails, at least fails while daring greatly."
President Theodore Roosevelt

It was scary being seen. Bruno inhaled and took one last look at Pops. Then he stepped up, spread the ropes, and he got in the ring.

Chapter 3

The Ring

"If you want the moon...
do not hide at night.
If you want a rose...
do not run from the thorns.
If you want love...
do not hide
from yourself."
Rumi

All alone on the canvas, Bruno started shadow boxing. Just a few minutes earlier he had felt about two feet tall. Now he felt almost 10 feet tall. The gym was coming to life as more people arrived, and seeing the place from this new perspective took some getting used to. Inside, Bruno negotiated the fine line between excitement and self-consciousness.

Bruno could hear someone singing and realized it was Pops. If a good song came on the radio, Pops always sang along. His voice sounded like the rich tones on the radio, and you could tell he loved music as much as boxing.

"Move around. Use the ring!" Pops beamed, stepping up and perching his forearms on the ropes. Still holding his tea, he said, "Move to the left..." And Bruno did, trying to get more graceful with his footwork. "Good. Now move to the right. Use the space," Pops said. "There you go!"

As Bruno moved around the ring, he started to relax a little, and the rest of the room fell away. He could hear Pops' voice and felt grateful that he was taking the time to help him. Under Pops' watchful gaze, Bruno felt protected, and he kept moving to get over his feelings of awkwardness.

"Don't worry about anyone else right now. Just you!" said Pops.

The longer Bruno forced himself into this uncomfortable space, the more comfortable he became. The more he concentrated on what he was doing, the less he heard the negative voices in his head.

Bruno finally stepped down, gloved up and did some work on the speed bag and heavy bag. *First, the ring! Now, the speed bag! He must be dreaming.*

On his way home from the gym that day, excited thoughts bounced through Bruno's mind, and his heart was racing. *I got in the ring,* he thought. *It was just to shadow box, but it was a step way outside my comfort zone. And I let myself be seen.*

Just then, as he passed by a shop window, he thought he saw the reflection of a boxer puppy with four white paws. But when he looked again, it was just his own reflection: an 18 year-old boy with fresh white socks.

Lying in bed that night, his room spare and moonlit, Bruno said Pops' pivotal words out loud. *Get in the ring.* That message floated into the night like a banner in the sky for him. Rather than wishing he could be a boxer, for the first time in his life he ended the day knowing he took a step in that direction.

He glanced up at the posters hanging on his wall. They were pictures of the boxing greats: Sugar Ray Robinson, Jack Dempsey and Jack Johnson. He wondered what their individual boxing journeys were like. He wondered about the struggles they faced inside and outside the ring. He wondered if they were ever scared to get in the ring. Bruno knew that to get to that level, they were either fearless, or they faced their fears one after another.

Then his eyes locked on the family photo in the worn wooden frame, and memories flooded his mind. He took a breath and walked out to the kitchen, and sitting under the glow of the ceiling light, he found his Mom reading at the small wooden table.

Chapter 4

The Key

"Continuous effort,
not strength or intelligence,
is the key to unlocking our potential."
Winston Churchill

"Mom?"

"Hey! How's my Bruno?" If voices could sparkle, hers did. That voice and that smile were Bruno's north star.

His Mom was a steady presence in his life. She was strong, yet easy-going: just the right amount protector, just the right amount friend. Her face was handsome, just like Bruno's, and at the same time, she was feminine and statuesque. Her life hadn't been easy, but she was always there for Bruno, and he thought of her as his number one earth angel. She was love personified. To Bruno, it made sense that her name was Grace.

Bruno wanted to tell his Mom about getting in the ring. As he searched for words, she could see the energy in his eyes, and she carefully marked her page and turned the book facedown on the table. Bruno was a quiet boy with deep thoughts, and when he was sharing something, she gave him her full attention. When he wanted to talk, he was speaking from his heart.

Bruno had never told his Mom about his fear of getting in the ring. He had been ashamed of it.

"I got in the ring today," said Bruno, pausing for a second. "And it was a big deal for me, Mom. I'm not sure I can really even explain it," he said, pulling in his chair.

"Okay," said his Mom, gently. "Go on…"

"I was practicing my shadow boxing on a low spot in the corner of the room. What I really wanted was to get up in the ring, but I was too scared. The next thing I knew, Pops was walking up to me, smiling and saying, 'Get in the ring.' Mom, those words hit me like a shot. Plus, hearing those words from Pops was especially powerful because I trust and admire and respect him more than I can even tell you. I not only heard, 'Get in the ring', you know, as in the actual boxing ring. I heard, 'Get back in the ring of life.'"

His Mom was silent. She put her hand on her heart, trying not to tear up. The depth this young boy showed from time to time left her in awe. She had been waiting for this day for years, wondering if it would ever come. After all, little Bruno had been through a lot in his young life. She could hear the pride in his voice, and her eyes began to shine.

"Here's what confuses me, Mom: Before I got in the ring, one part of me was feeling really good and motivated, and another part of me was feeling angry and ashamed for being too scared to get in the ring. Is that kind of inner conflict just part of being human? Am I making any sense?"

"Yes, you make perfect sense…" she said.

Bruno let out a big sigh. "I don't know what's happening in me, but something happened when I got in the ring. I feel optimistic. I feel hopeful. I feel good. And for the first time in a long time, I don't feel invisible."

Invisible. His Mom's heart hurt to know Bruno had been feeling invisible. She reached her hands across the table and held Bruno's.

"Not everyone is going to get us. And when we care about that, it can make us feel invisible. But these good feelings you're having right now: that's what happens when you start living your truth. Not everyone is going to like it, and not everyone is going to get it. That doesn't matter. What matters is you feel in sync with yourself and with the people you respect. They become your tribe. You will feel energized. You will feel focused. And you will feel at peace."

She remembered the simple necklace hanging around her neck and touched the tiny charm. "To your question about inner conflict: There is one thing that I wish I'd understood when I was younger. In my opinion, it is the key to working through inner conflict, the key to freedom and the key to unlocking our highest potential."

"What is it, Mom?" asked Bruno, looking at his Mom's key pendant. The chain was so delicate, the key seemed to float between her collar bones.

"I wish I had known we have the power to choose our thoughts. For me, this is not done in a heavy-handed way. I find it most helpful to take a gentle way. It starts by going within. I realize I can separate a little. I can observe my thoughts without attaching to them. If I observe that my thoughts are preventing me from being my whole self, or if I observe that my thoughts are hurting me or making me feel physically unwell, or if I observe that my thoughts are taking me in the opposite direction of my dreams… I pause. I take a breath. I take as many breaths as I need to quiet my thoughts. And in that moment, I remind myself I can choose to think in a new way. Changing my thoughts changes how I feel. Changing how I feel changes my energy. And changing my energy changes my world.

"The conflict you experienced this morning is an example of how our thoughts can impact our emotions and our actions. Negative thinking keeps us from getting in the ring. Positive thinking gives us the courage to step up. How we think changes everything, Bruno. Everything. With gentle but disciplined thinking, we can focus on who we want to be and what we want to do, and we can move in the direction of our truth, our joy and our dreams."

"So what we *think* is connected to how we *feel* and what we *do*?" asked Bruno.

"Yes. One hundred percent. If we think loving thoughts, we will likely act in loving ways. If we think angry thoughts, we will likely act in angry ways. How we think directs how we show up in the world. That's why we need to be careful about what kinds of things we let into our minds and into our lives. We need to tend to our thoughts and keep them healthy, strong and loving," she smiled, sitting up a little straighter.

"So today when Pops said, 'Get in the ring,' he helped change my thinking, and he did it in a gentle way?" said Bruno.

"That's right. Sometimes the gentle redirection comes from outside. But more often, it needs to come from inside you, Bruno. Sometimes it will feel like a real struggle to turn your thoughts around. But you can do it. It's a choice. For each and every person, it is a choice."

"Okay. I'll try to observe my thoughts and remember they don't have to control me. I guess I wasn't really aware of that. I guess I just unconsciously accepted all of my thoughts as truth. And I guess I just thought I had to feel the way they made me feel. It's kind of a relief to hear that I have a role to play in my thoughts, and I can control them rather than the other way around. Thanks for this, Mom, and thanks for listening to me tonight," he said, looking up at the clock. It was already 11:11pm. Bruno had heard 11:11 was an auspicious sign, so he chose to believe it and smiled.

"Of course. I love you," she said giving him a hug. "And I'm proud of you." Looking Bruno in the eye, she said, "You remember what to do, right?" She always asked him this question.

"Yes, Mom," he said. "Trust myself."

"That's right. I raised you right, and you have good instincts. Now trust yourself," she said.

"Thanks, Mom," said Bruno, grinning his shy crooked grin. "Nite."

Back on his bed and looking at the pictures again, Bruno felt nostalgic. He remembered that last road trip with his Mom and Dad in the old Chevy. And there he was, winning some kind of prize at the science fair in third grade.

And there, on the end, was the photo of Bruno with the officer who took him home after he was caught stealing from the store. Bruno will remember that day forever. The next thing he knew, his Mom told him to put on his gym shorts, sneakers and a t-shirt. Together, they took a drive, parked and walked into the boxing gym. That's where it all began.

Chapter 5

Grit

"The only way out is through."
Robert Frost

"C'mon dig. Dig!" said Pops, holding mitts as targets for Bruno. Bruno threw a left uppercut, a right uppercut, a left uppercut. "Don't stop!"

Bruno had good form, good speed and increasingly good power. But he had poor stamina. He was running out of gas.

Ding! Ding! Ding! The bell.

Oh, thank you! said Bruno, looking up. He was relieved to have a 30 second break between rounds. Pops pulled off his mitts and grabbed a water bottle. As Bruno tipped his head back to drink, Pops reminded him, "You have to breathe, son. You have to remember to breathe."

"I'm holding my breath again, huh?" Bruno asked.

"Yep." said Pops. "In through your nose and out through your mouth," he said. Bruno slowed his breathing and took one more sip of water. The bell rang, and they walked to the middle of the ring.

"Jab," said Pops. "Jab. Jab. Double jab." They did combinations as they moved around the ring. The work tested Bruno's physical abilities, and it was mentally challenging too. Pops kept simple and complex combinations in his head like a comedian keeps a file cabinet of jokes, and his memory for technique and drills was encyclopedic. Patient and thoughtful, being in the ring together with his fighters gave Pops a perspective on them that no one else could see.

Pops and Bruno moved closer to the edge of the ring, and Bruno's back was against the ropes. Whenever this happened, Pops could see that anger would flare up inside of Bruno.

"Focus, Bruno," said Pops. "Block and counter and get around."

On the ropes, Bruno felt trapped, and it created a panic in him that showed up as anger. Anger made Bruno feel momentarily powerful, and then very quickly, powerless. He needed to find a new way. He tried to remember his Dad's boxing principles: *We can be victims or we can be fighters. We can spin out of control or we can learn to be still. We can get frustrated or we can get focused.*

Bruno took a breath, and he observed. *You're on the ropes. Okay. What are you going to do? Find a way out.*

Something shifted in Bruno. Epiphanies and breakthroughs are like that. They sneak up on you when you're taking action on your dream and walking through pain or uncertainty. He started to redirect his thinking from panic to curiosity to action. *You can get off the ropes.*

"Work through it, B!" said Pops. "It doesn't have to be pretty. You can do it!" Pops kept their pad work on the ropes so Bruno would have to find a solution.

What do I need to do? thought Bruno. If he expected to do anything in the ring or anywhere else, he knew he needed to conquer himself first. Pops believed in him. Now Bruno needed to believe in himself.

"Bruno, go!" said Pops.

And he went! Bruno blocked and countered and got around. He was under and out and back in the center of the ring. He was no longer on the ropes.

"Ahh!" Pops' arms shot into the air and his face lit up. "Yes!" beamed Pops. "Yes! See? It's amazing. When you believe you can, you do! That's my boy!"

Bruno's eyes shined too. For the first time in his life, he fought against anger with thoughtfulness and calm, and he won.

Feeling great about the day, Bruno packed up to head home. As he was leaving the gym, Pops said, "Bruno, what have you done for your Mom lately?"

Bruno's eyes darted into space, an attempt at avoiding the question.

"Do something for your Mom! At very least, let her know how much you appreciate her. Okay?"

"Okay, Coach. I will."

"You better!"

"Okay," laughed Bruno. "I will! I will!"

That evening, Bruno reflected on the day. He knew he had to learn to manage his anger better, but he was proud of his breakthrough. It was the first time in a long time that he didn't let his anger spin out of control, and it felt good.

Energized, he decided to go for a run in the hills. He remembered Pops telling him to spend time in nature every day. "Nature has a way of smoothing out our edges, and it revitalizes us," Pops told him. "All it takes is a walk outside to understand that spending time in nature elevates us spiritually, physically and emotionally. It stirs inspiration and creative thought."

As he ran, Bruno counted his latest blessings. First, he got in the ring. Then, he started to react differently when he was on the ropes. Now, he was figuring out how to use his anger more constructively. He'd been living on autopilot for too long, and he wanted to start living his life on purpose, with intention. He knew it was time to face his fears. His Mom had told him, "Facing your fear is an act of love. You have to love yourself to face your fear."

Bruno felt the fresh air on his skin as he ran in silence through the late golden light. Accompanied by the steady sound of his breath, his legs felt strong and his spirits were high. *I need a goal,* thought Bruno as he ran. *I need some kind of goal.* He pushed hard when he ran up the hills, and on the flat open canyon trails, he stretched out his stride. *But what goal?*

He was getting loose, and he found a rhythm in his run. All the while, snapshots from training played in his mind. The flashes of glimmering sunlight, the gold, the white, Pops saying, "Get in the ring," shadow boxing, hitting the mitts, the heavy bag and speed bag. It was a beautiful blur, and Bruno felt like he was flying.

I know! That's it! He jumped over a log and let out a *Woo!* that sounded like an odd howl. Something about being out there alone, moving in nature, made him feel invincible.

The thought of this goal scared Bruno and thrilled him at the same time. His Mom always told him to listen for small whispers of intuition and dreams. She said that when that small voice inside you speaks a dream into your consciousness, if you feel an honest mix of fear and excitement, that is how the universe tells us, *Yes, you must try it.*

Chapter 6

The Goal

"I learned what every dreaming child needs to know,
that no horizon is so far you cannot get above it or beyond it."
Beryl Markham

The sun was barely up and a new day had begun. Pops was already at the gym when Bruno burst in full of life. "Coach! Coach!" he said, running up to Pops.

Pops greeted Bruno with a hug and a smile. "Good morning, young man!" said Pops, in his easy, pleasant way. "How you doing?"

"Coach!" burst Bruno. "I want to know what you think. I was running in the canyon last night, and I realized I need a goal. And my goal is this: I want to train for an amateur fight!" Bruno said, eyes wide. "I want you to help me get in the ring for real, Coach. I need you."

Pops thought back to the day Bruno got in the ring to shadow box for the first time. It seemed so long ago now. Bruno had grown so much.

"Okay," said Pops slowly. "First, I think it's great that you have decided to give yourself a goal. But let me ask you a question. Apart from wanting to have a goal, why do you want to train for a fight? This isn't for everyone. You can train and you can work hard without having to fight or even spar. That's okay. So why do you choose this goal?"

Bruno looked at the ground and then looked back up into Pops' eyes.

"Number one, I love boxing. It makes me feel good. Number two, I'm tired of living scared. I'm tired of worrying about what everyone else thinks. Boxing just keeps calling me and tugging at me. There's something in me, Coach, and it won't go away. So I need to see about it. I just feel like this is something I need to do. If I don't try this, if I don't challenge myself in this way, I know I'll regret it."

Pops was listening. For the first time, he could see Bruno showing qualities of personal leadership.

"I think if I can do this, it will help me in so many other ways. Worrying about what people think of me holds me back here at the gym and outside the gym too. Training with you is helping me with that. Your singing woke me up to that! You sing and let anyone hear. I want to be like that. By getting in the ring, by following your guidance and example, I'm starting to feel stronger. Physically, yeah, but the bigger changes are happening in here, and up here," said Bruno, pointing to his heart then his head. "All of this is giving me some self-confidence. And little by little, I spend less energy worrying about what other people think of me. I need more of that."

Pops could tell this was a thoughtful decision by Bruno. Knowing Bruno's talent and true potential, Pops nodded his head slowly.

"Okay. If that's what you want to do, you have to be prepared to do what it takes."

Bruno was hanging on his every word. Since having the thought the night before, everything else seemed to fall away for Bruno. The idea arrived in a whisper, but once realized, the necessity of this goal hit like a flash of inspiration so bright it was dizzying. There was nothing else he wanted to do. He felt giddy, driven and energized.

"You can't partially commit," said Pops. "You need to make up your mind to train hard. You need to show up. You need to push yourself," continued Pops. "Most of all, you have to really want it. You are going to have days when this won't be fun at all. I'm not going to sugarcoat it. You can't just be in love with the *idea* of this. You need to be in love with the *reality* of this."

He let that sink in for a minute, and Bruno's wide eyes didn't blink. They looked at each other for a long moment.

"But you're tough, and you're talented, and you're smart. And if you have made up your mind that this is what you want to do, I'll help you."

Bruno sprung forward and gave Pops a hug so big that it wobbled his balance, like a puppy who doesn't know his own strength.

"Whoa!" laughed Pops. He had never seen Bruno so excited.

"Thank you, Coach! Thank you!" said Bruno.

"Okay, okay!" laughed Pops, pushing him off. "Get off me. Knucklehead!"

Bruno felt a rush of love and joy. Pops called over to him.

"Okay. C'mon, son! Let's do this."

Chapter 7

The Team

*"We are not a team because we work
together. We are a team because
we respect, trust, and care for each other."*
Vala Afshar

From that moment on, Bruno and Pops trained together six
days a week. In the early dawn hours, before the rest of the world
was up, they would meet, either in the gym or in the park, for an
early run. The fight date would approach soon enough, and they
needed to be ready.

Heavy bag. Push ups. Mitt work. Double end bag. Footwork.
Defensive work. Speed bag. Abs. In the process of his training,
Bruno was more observant of his thoughts than ever. And he was
learning to gently redirect them when they were creating anxiety,
anger or doubt.

In addition to his work with Pops, Bruno also worked with a
strength and conditioning coach named Bear. No one knew his real
name but his burly badge suited him. Bear taught Bruno about
nutrition and food portions too. Bruno needed to be ready on fight
night, and that not only meant being able to bring his best boxing
skills and mindset, but also a strong and fit body that would come in
on weight.

One day, after an evening training session, Bruno, Pops and
Bear were sitting around together in the gym, talking and
rehydrating. All of a sudden, Bruno looked at Bear and asked him
about his name.

"How'd you get that name: Bear?" Bruno took a drink from his water bottle with a B on it.

"Well, isn't it obvious?" Bear stood proud and puffed out his chest. Bruno and Pops dropped their heads to stifle their laughs.

"Kind of," said Bruno, looking up again. Squinting his eyes, he said, "Yeah, I can see it." He turned to look at Pops. "Can you see it, Coach?"

"He's no bear," said Pops. "Maybe a teddy bear!" They all laughed.

"For real," said Bear. "The bear is my spirit animal..."

"See!" said Pops.

"Really! It's my spirit animal. Somewhere along the line, I just sort of adopted it as my name," said Bear.

"Well, does it have a deeper meaning?" asked Bruno.

"It sure does! First of all, it means I'm very handsome." Pops and Bruno rolled their eyes this time. "And!" Bear continued, "It means I am strong. I can use my abilities to help heal others. My very best quality: I know the importance of rest. I hibernate for eight hours every night!"

Bruno laughed.

"Don't laugh! There is nothing macho about not getting enough rest. We need sleep to perform at our best. Listen to the Bear! The Bear knows!"

"Well, what is Pops' spirit animal?" asked Bruno. Bear tilted his head sideways and thought for a minute, taking a good look at Coach. His eyes lit up.

"Yours would be an owl!" said Bear, pointing toward Pops and looking pleased with himself. "Yours would be an owl because owls are wise, and they see things others cannot!" said Bear. He was feeling energized now. These guys were indulging him in the kind of philosophical conversation he loved.

"Also, you have high intuition, and you see truth!" Bear looked like he rested his case.

"Whoa," said Bruno, his eyes like saucers looking from Bear to Pops. "He's right, Coach!"

Pops raised his eyebrows and laughed a beat, touched by this praise.

"What about me?" asked Bruno. "What is mine?"

Bear and Pops both looked at Bruno, thinking.

"Hmm. Maybe a wolf, because the wolf is sharp, has good instincts and wants to be free," said Bear. But he was still deciding if a wolf was the right animal.

"How about a boxer dog?" said Pops. "He's energetic, intelligent, brave."

"Yes!" said Bear, standing up again. "That's it! And add to that loyal. And a truth seeker. One who is becoming his true self."

Pops nodded big, saying, "Yep. That's it. That's our Bruno!"

Bruno felt something powerful wash over him. He felt like Pops and Bear had just seen his soul.

"A boxer…" said Bruno, barely audible. His skin started to tingle and his white socks glimmered like stars.

"Yes, son! A boxer!" said Pops, putting his hand on Bruno's shoulder as he stood up. "So tomorrow, I'm bringing Max in to move around with you. We'll do some light sparring and get that first day out of the way. Good? Good!"

Bruno knew this day would come. He'd have to spar for the first time some time.

"Good work today, B. See you tomorrow," said Pops. "Nite Bear!"

"Nite, Coach!" they said in unison.

Chapter 8

The Test

"I learned that courage was not the absence of fear,
but the triumph over it.
The brave man is not he who does not feel afraid,
but he who conquers that fear."
Nelson Mandela

It was already warm in the gym even though it was still early in the morning. Or maybe it was just that Bruno's adrenaline was racing. Pops, focused on wrapping Bruno's hands, asked him, "How do you feel?"

"Ready to get this first one out of the way, to be honest," said Bruno.

"I hear you. You'll be all right. Use what you know. You've been training hard," said Pops. He finished wrapping Bruno's hands. "Nothing intense today. Move around, stay loose and trust yourself," said Pops.

Bruno laughed a little. "Why are you laughing?" smiled Pops.

"That's what my Mom always says to me. She tells me she raised me right, and to trust myself," said Bruno, cracking a grin.

"Well, she's right!" said Pops. "Listen to your Mom. Speaking of your Mom, what have you done for her lately?"

"Um." Bruno knew he was about to get scolded.

"Help your Mom, B! Clean up around the house without her asking. Show her you care about her," said Pops. "I'm going to keep after you until you do."

"I know. I know. I will!" said Bruno, smiling now. Coach was right.

Just then the door opened, and Max walked in. "Hey, Max," said Pops. "Good morning."

"Hi Coach. Good morning!" said Max. "Hi Bruno. We'll have fun today," he said tapping Bruno's shoulder, sincerely. He knew Bruno was nervous and wanted to put him at ease. "How do you feel?"

"Good. Good," said Bruno, trying to convince himself. He stretched, shadow boxed and took a deep breath. He reminded himself that this was his choice. He reminded himself that this was a necessary step on the way to his bigger goal. And he reminded himself that the discomfort he was feeling was a measure of growth that comes with change and a new challenge.

Pops helped Bruno into his gloves and headgear, and everything after that is a bit of a blur for Bruno. He knew he got in the ring, and he made it back out again. What happened in the middle was fuzzy.

With Pops in his corner, Bruno felt strong and supported. Bruno and Max did four three-minute rounds of sparring, with a one minute break between each round. Bruno was winded in a way he hadn't experienced before, and he found sparring to be a whole different level of engagement. His heart was pounding.

In the ring that day, Bruno landed a few shots on Max, but Bruno got caught with a few too. They weren't particularly hard, but the first ones stunned him a little. His nose bled, and the body shots that followed made him realize he needed to focus like never before. The hits, the panic, the recovery — this was all a new feeling for him. But Bruno was holding his own, and he realized the fear he anticipated before getting in the ring was so much worse than the reality of being in the ring. His attitude, his focus and his adrenaline pushed fear away with every exchange, and his training served him well. He was right where he wanted to be. It wasn't supposed to be easy.

After the last bell, Bruno and Max hugged. Breathless, Bruno returned to his corner, filled with relief. Pops helped remove Bruno's mouth piece and gave him a hug.

"I'm proud of you, son. You got in the ring," said Pops, smiling.

"Thanks, Coach. For everything!" said Bruno.

"You're welcome," said Pops.

Bruno felt exhilarated, exhausted and proud of himself. As he walked to the door that day, Bruno heard Pops' authoritative voice. "Your Mom! Remember, Bruno!"

Bruno looked back, smiled and nodded. "I got it, Coach! I promise!" he said. Bruno felt seen. He felt appreciated. He felt loved.

Chapter 9

Reflection

"If you want to understand the Universe,
think of energy, frequency and vibration."
Nikola Tesla

Bruno took his time walking home. He inhaled the sun shining through the leafy green trees and barely noticed the passing cars. He was thinking about what happened in the ring, and he changed his gait with the images in his mind. Bruno felt humbled and possessed a steady calm. Sparring was something he had only dreamed of doing, and now he felt a new and profound sense of accomplishment and purpose.

He was so grateful his Mom had taken him to the boxing gym all those years ago. He admired her quiet strength. *Trust yourself.* He heard her words and felt her love, but he rarely made that known. Coach was right. He needed to communicate it, not just think it and feel it.

He took out his cellphone and dialed. Bruno could hear his Mom smiling.

"How's my Bruno?" she said.

"I'm good!" he sighed. "I'm really good, Mom," he said, speaking in time with his slow steps. "I'm on my way home from the gym. How are you?" he asked.

It had been a long time since Bruno had asked his Mom how she was doing, and upon hearing those words, her clear voice turned velvety. "I'm good, too," she said warmly. "I'm good, too, B."

"Good. Mom, I did something today! Something I had been scared to do…" Bruno shared.

"What did you do?" Her question sounded like a statement, and her voice was filled with tenderness.

"I sparred, Mom," said Bruno. "I got in the ring for real."

"Wow. Okay. And how did it feel?" she asked.

"It felt so good! I mean, at times it didn't, but overall, it felt great!" he said. "I was nervous all morning. And I know I was kind of clumsy in there. But I felt good. Pops brought in a guy named Max as my opponent. I know he held back some, but he didn't make it easy either.

"The mental and physical work I have been doing with Pops, combined with the strength and conditioning drills I've done with Bear, all helped me get in the ring feeling ready. I have more to do, but it was a good start," he said.

"Congratulations! I'm so proud of you!" she said.

"Mom, I'm not sure where I'd be without you."

He thought about how they had lost his Dad. He thought about getting in trouble at the store. He thought about how he withdrew from everyone including his Mom. He thought about how many times they had moved. He thought about how hard his Mom worked.

"I was so young when Dad got sick," continued Bruno. "When we lost him, life felt so unfair. I didn't know who to be or how to be. And since I was just a kid, I didn't realize you were grieving, too, Mom. You were so strong that my young mind and broken heart didn't see your pain, your grief and your fight for our survival. But I see it now.

"I know I started making bad decisions. And I know I made things even harder for you. But you were there for me. And I am so grateful, Mom. One of the best things you ever did was make me go to the boxing gym. Through boxing, I feel like I can finally breathe again. I am starting to understand that message on your book marker, the one by Michael B. Beckwith: '*Pain pushes until vision pulls.*' I think I get it now."

A car honked as Bruno was about to cross the street. It was Max, waving and giving Bruno a peace sign.

"I'm not sure how I turned my boxing experience today into all of this," Bruno said, waving back at Max. "I guess it just stirred up a lot in me, things that aren't even related to boxing." Bruno sounded a little puzzled.

"I think it's all related. And there are no right or wrong paths in our conversations. You can jump from boxing to your Dad to whatever you like," his Mom said. "It makes sense to me that this is all coming up right now. One moving part in life affects all the parts. Going deep in one area of life will usually cause us to go deep in other areas. For example, when we change our exercise, we impact our sleep. Or when we improve our nutrition, our bodies become healthier. When we feel better about ourselves, that affects our relationships. And so on. It's all connected.

"So by pursing your passion at the gym and putting so much of your heart and soul into something you love, you are stirring other depths in your heart and soul. You have taken a very hard thing — the pain of losing your Dad — and you are channeling it in a positive way now. In the process, you are discovering who you are, what drives you and what kind of person you want to become.

"Life isn't fair sometimes. But you know what? You kept going. We kept going. We are fighters. And right now I see so many good things in you, I can't even quite express. You are a fine young man, Bruno, and your Dad would be so proud of you. I am so proud of you..." she trailed off.

"Now! Let's get back to where we started: You sparred today, baby! You created a challenge for yourself, and you stepped to it. Congratulations!"

Then Bruno heard a big *Muah!* sound through the phone, and he snorted a laugh.

"Hahaha. Thank you, Mom!" he flushed. "Thank you. I'll be home soon." He smiled and ended the call.

Just then, a small butterfly flew in front of Bruno and landed on a purple wildflower growing near the edge of the sidewalk. As soon as it touched down, it flew away again.

The flower swayed ever so slightly. "*I got it, Coach,*" thought Bruno, shaking his head, smiling. He reached down to take the flower home to his Mom.

Chapter 10

The Chatter

"Your time is limited, so don't waste it living someone else's life. Don't be trapped by dogma — which is living with the results of other people's thinking. Don't let the noise of others' opinions drown out your own inner voice. And most important, have the courage to follow your heart and intuition."
Steve Jobs

After months of hard training and discipline, Bruno had begun to carry himself differently. He had an aura about him now that was a mixture of confidence, humility and maturity. He had come through a lot of tough sparring sessions, bloody and bruised. And even though there were days when he didn't think he had anything left, he kept showing up.

But one morning, when Bruno was barely awake, he found what felt like every single member of the negative committee sitting there at the bottom of his bed. He could hear their chatter even before he'd opened his eyes. *Who do you think you are? You can't be a boxer. You're not good enough.*

Bruno flipped over onto his stomach and put the pillow over his head. But the chatter continued. He'd felt so good when he went to sleep. *Why this? Why now?*

The bedroom door squeaked, and his Mom whispered through the crack. "Morning. Who is the sleepy head today? Don't you have to get to the gym?"

Bruno turned over and managed to say he and Pops were training a little later today.

"Okay. Do you want some breakfast?" she asked.

"Okay. I'll be there in just a minute. Thanks, Ma," he said. He heard the door close then dropped his legs over the edge of his bed. He sat for a second, pushing the heels of his hands into his closed eyes. He looked down at his tall white socks and tried to quiet the chatter, then glanced up at the posters of the boxing greats on his wall.

I have to get up, he thought.

On the table, his Mom made a colorful plate of healthy food: a large omelet with ground turkey, vegetables and some fruit. As Bruno sat down, he inhaled the scent of toast as his Mom opened the windows over the sink, letting in a ribbon of fresh air. She was wearing a plain white t-shirt and loose jeans, her long hair swirled into a high bun.

"How are you this morning?" she smiled at Bruno as she sat down.

Bruno shook his head a little, shrugged and looked down at his food. "I don't know, Mom. Maybe I'm not meant to be a boxer," he said quietly.

"Wait a minute," she said, calmly setting down her fork. "Bruno, where is this coming from?"

Bruno shrugged again. "I don't know."

"Okay," she said. "Do you still enjoy going to the gym?"

"Yes."

"Have you learned a lot since you started training?"

"Yes."

"Do you feel good when you are boxing?"

"Yes."

"Has it felt good to be working toward a goal?"

"Yes."

"Is everyone at the gym being cool?"

"Yes."

"Do you still love boxing?"

"Yes."

They sat in silence for a moment, and his Mom took a sip of coffee, studying him. Then she realized something.

"Your fight is coming up soon," she said, thoughtfully.

"Mhm," said Bruno, nodding.

"How are you feeling about that?" She was treading softly.

Bruno shrugged. "Good, I guess. Nervous. Mostly nervous," he admitted.

"Okay. That's natural, you know. Feeling nervous and having doubt in advance of doing anything we really care about is normal. It's that fear thing we've talked about. You're going to do great in your fight. Just go out there and give your very best effort.

"We tend to get paralyzed if we think we have to do everything perfectly. One thing I know is that our best will vary from day to day. Still, we must aim for consistency and improvement. Still, we must give our best effort. For me, sometimes that best effort looks like stumbling through," she laughed.

"But if we really want something, we need to do it nervous. We need to do it scared. We need to do it anyway. If we aren't willing to do it, then maybe we don't really want it. If we do, we'll do it anyway."

Bruno nodded. He knew he wanted this.

"Do you remember how you felt when you set your goal in the first place? Harness energy from that. And proceed," she smiled.

Bruno knew he had been training hard, eating right and sleeping enough. And he had even heard the chatter of the committee at the bottom of his bed before, and he managed to fight them off.

"Sometimes I look around and realize how far I have to go to be a great boxer, and I wonder what I am even doing," said Bruno.

His Mom gave him a loving look with bright eyes, tilting her head up, hoping it would make Bruno's chin come up too.

"Your aim should be to enjoy the process. You may not have as far to go as you think. Instead of focusing on what isn't yet, focus on what is. Be grateful for the blessings you've been given, and be curious about the blessings you are yet to receive. Take this moment, right now, and look at how far you've come. Give yourself some credit. It's okay. Then go do your dreams."

Bruno sat there for a moment, deep in thought, then he looked up at his Mom.

"I don't want to look silly out there, Ma. I don't want to hear people say I'm no good. I want to inspire young guys and be a role model. I want to have a great night for me, and I want to make you and Pops and Bear proud," said Bruno. "All of you have supported me in this dream. Today, I just woke up filled with self-doubt and all the chatter from the committee at the bottom of my bed was louder than ever, you know?"

His Mom knew. Every time she identified something she really wanted in life, an inexplicable wave of self-doubt would show up. It was a formidable foe that would catch her by surprise. But then she would remember her necklace and the symbolism it held.

"First, you're not going to look silly. You're going to be great. But the point is: it doesn't matter. Remember that piece of paper you carry in your pocket? Look at it for support when you need a reminder. What matters is you're in the ring. What matters is you're living your truth. What other people think, and what the committee says: give them no weight. They are just thoughts. Remember?"

"That's the key, huh?" said Bruno, looking at his Mom's necklace. "Just like when I wanted to get in the ring to shadow box, I let my negative thoughts keep me from stepping up until Pops came by and encouraged me to get in the ring."

"Yes! That's right. And when you realize your negative thoughts, you can choose to think in a new way, right? It sounds like this morning you woke up to a runaway train of negative thoughts. I'm glad we are talking about it because it takes away their power and helps us get back on track," she smiled.

His Mom was like a magic reset button.

"What really matters here is you and your mindset. I know that in the world of boxing, there is an actual opponent. But you have to meet yourself first, in quiet moments like this, in your pajamas. Those posters you have on your wall are there for a reason, aren't they?" she asked. "Why are they there?"

Bruno stared at his Mom, thinking.

"Those guys are the greats, Mom. They inspire me. I want to be like them."

"That's right," she continued. "And it's easy think the people who are on top in any field got there without struggle. No way. The bottom line is they are survivors. It doesn't mean they didn't get knocked down. It doesn't mean they didn't think about giving up. It doesn't mean they didn't wake up one morning and feel like they weren't good enough. I guarantee you, they all did. The difference is they kept going. They tried again. And again. And again.

"So, tell that committee to stuff it. Write it on your heart that you will be the best Bruno of all time. There is no one like you. It's time to step into your own greatness, B."

"Thank you. I appreciate you, Mom," said Bruno.

"I appreciate you too, B!" she said, eyes gleaming.

Chapter 11

Weigh-In Day

*"Life's most persistent and urgent question is,
What are you doing for others?"*
Martin Luther King, Jr.

Weigh-in day arrived, and when Bruno stepped on the scale, he was right where he needed to be. Afterward, Pops and Bruno sat down together for lunch. It was time to eat, hydrate then rest. The big day was tomorrow.

"I can't believe it's almost here, Coach," said Bruno. "Remember the day you told me to get in the ring? That day changed everything for me. You made me feel visible. You made me feel like I belonged. You made me feel like you saw potential in me that I didn't see in myself."

"I did see potential in you, Bruno," said Pops. "You were finally ready to see it, too."

Bruno reached for a napkin.

"You had been eyeing the ring for a long time, and I could see you wanted to get up there. I didn't know that you would decide to train for a fight, but I knew you wanted to get in the ring."

"Did I ever tell you why my Mom took me to the gym for the first time, Coach?" asked Bruno. "When I was about 10 or 11 years old, a police officer caught me trying to steal a toy car from the store, and when my Mom found out, she was *mad*. My Mom doesn't get mad. But she was *mad*! She didn't say a single word, Coach! She stood still as a statue, her eyes staring through me like lasers!"

Pops laughed. Sometimes Bruno was still a boy, and it was endearing.

"It was the worst feeling ever, Coach. Then she made me get in the car, and we drove to the gym. I didn't really know why I was there at first, but now it's starting to make sense. She brought me there to punish me," said Bruno.

"No, knucklehead!" laughed Pops. "She didn't bring you there to punish you! She brought you there to save you!"

Bruno looked at Pops and tilted his head a little.

"Look," said Pops. "I have known you since you were just a pup, even before you remember. I knew your Dad. He was a boxer, too, did you know that?"

Bruno nodded his head yes. "Wow. I didn't know you knew him," said Bruno.

"I sure did. He was my friend. He was a great man, and a great boxer, too. After you lost your Dad, your Mom knew how much you were hurting. And then after the stealing incident, she was worried you were headed down a bad road. She wanted to give you a place and an activity that would keep you out of trouble. So she brought you to the gym. She knew your Dad and I were friends, so she asked me to keep an eye on you."

"She did?" Bruno's eyes were wide.

"Yes, she did. And I have been keeping an eye on you ever since. I hoped boxing would help you like it did your Dad and me and so many other people. I have followed my passion and I have made my passion my life's work. I have met wonderful people. I have traveled the world. And most of all, I've tried to be of service. I've tried to help young guys, like you, believe in yourself.

"I don't care if you pursue boxing. What I want is for you to have the courage to pursue your heart's desires and to be a good person. Seeing you guys shine in your life is the greatest gift I could ever receive. The benefits of giving far outweigh the benefits of receiving, Bruno. That's part of the reason I'm always encouraging you to do things for your Mom. I want you to feel that.

"Sometimes people associate service with doing for strangers. Well, yes. But we should also be of service to those who are closest to us. It doesn't require money. It just requires a little creativity and a lot of love. Plus, you just need to remind your Mom you love her and appreciate her sometimes. She deserves that."

Bruno looked at his hands, then at Pops.

"You're right, Coach. I'm getting better at that, thanks to you. And I just want to say, never doubt the impact you have had on me. Not only are you a great trainer and have more talent and knowledge than you'd ever say, you have taught me so much about boxing, about integrity and about life. Your example speaks volumes. I see how you carry yourself. You're strong, but you're kind. You're serious, but you're silly. You're world-class, but you're humble. I love you, Coach."

"I love you too, son. You're going to be all right. Tomorrow night, do what you know. When you get in the ring, it's your whole body and your whole mind in the ring. Be fully present."

"I'm ready, Coach. Thank you!"

"You're welcome, Bruno. Today, tomorrow night and always, I'm in your corner."

Chapter 12

Fight Night

*"You never know which door will lead you
towards your dreams
until you have the courage
to walk through it."*
Unknown

Bruno arrived at the venue on his own, and he saw Pops pulling into the parking lot at the same time. As Pops shut his car door, he called to Bruno. "Hey, Champ!" he said, draping his arm over Bruno's shoulder. "How do you feel?"

"I feel good, Coach. Let's do this!" smiled Bruno, using Coach's words.

They walked inside together, and after the necessary paperwork was completed, Bruno and Pops got changed, stretched and warmed up in the back room.

When Pops was wrapping Bruno's hands, Bruno looked up at a poster hanging on the wall nearby. It was a picture of a Broadway performer, and it said: *No trumpets sound when the important decisions of our life are made. Destiny is made known silently.*
AGNES DE MILLE

Bruno looked at Pops.

"That makes me think of something my Mom told me one morning at breakfast when I was struggling with self-doubt and worrying about other people's opinions. She said, '*You have to meet yourself first, in quiet moments like this, in your pajamas.*'"

Pops chuckled. "I like that. You ought to put that on a poster for your Mom. *'You have to meet yourself first, in quiet moments like this, in your pajamas.' GRACE .*"

They laughed, and just then Bear arrived. He spoke as if he was making a grand theater entrance:

"*'If my mind can conceive it, and my heart can believe it, then I can achieve it…'*"

At the same time, Bear, Pops and Bruno finished that thought. "*MUHAMMAD ALI!*" they said in unison, then broke into laughter.

Bruno's Mom popped her head in to give Bruno a hug and to tell him good luck. After she left, Bruno noticed she'd placed a tiny key on the chair next to him. She had such subtle ways of getting through to him. Bruno knew she was saying, *'Remember the key.'* Bruno closed his eyes for a second, took a deep breath and checked his thoughts.

"Coach," said Bruno. "I feel like I should be more nervous, but for some reason, I feel all right," he said, looking up at Pops.

"That's because you've been doing the work. You're focused. You have your head and your heart in the right place. Now, go out there, and do your best. Okay?" said Pops.

"Okay, Coach!" said Bruno.

The next thing Bruno knew, he was getting in the ring and Pops was right behind him. The crowd was alive, and Bruno could feel their energy. Under the heat of the lights shining bright, Bruno took off his sweatshirt. There he stood in his shiny brown and white boxing trunks, white socks and white lace-up boxing gloves. It was time.

Bruno shook out his arms and legs as his eyes stayed fixed in a comfortable gaze on the distant canvas. He was focused. He felt Pops' strong hand on his shoulder, and his confidence surged. *I'm doing this,* he thought. He was in the ring. He was visible. He was moving through space and time motivated by love, not fear.

When the announcer called Bruno and his opponent to the center of the ring where the referee would give the final fight instructions, Bruno and Pops walked out together. The lights felt even brighter in the center of the ring. Bruno could feel the crowd's eyes on him, but he kept his eyes fixed on the ground. His ears were alert, and he listened intently to the referee's instructions to fight a clean fight. Then the referee told the fighters to touch gloves.

Bruno took a deep breath, and as he lifted his eyes to look at his opponent, the world moved in slow motion. Confetti of gold and white light spun down all around them like luminous rain. Bruno reached out his gloves, and he locked eyes with his opponent.

Bruno was looking at himself.

Chapter 13

Waking Up

*"You realize that all along
there was something tremendous
within you,
and you did not know it."*
Paramahansa Yogananda

The guys in the gym gathered around the silly puppy they loved so much. Laying in a bright strip of sun, Bruno had fallen asleep, and he must have been having some kind of doggie dream. His little legs were running, and he was panting. His little paws were moving, and it even looked like his head was bobbing and weaving.

"Bruno, are you having a dream? Huh?" asked Pops.

The puppy's eyes popped open, and he jumped up to his feet, startled. One of his ears was still flopped over as he looked up at Pops, scanned the room of people and then ran over to the wooden platform. He slipped across the paint and slid to a stop in front of the mirror.

As he stared at his reflection, he saw a white spark fly off his paw. He took a couple of breaths then blinked. He couldn't believe his eyes. He understood.

Inside this little puppy body with uneven white socks and floppy ears, there was a boxer.

Bruno was a boxer. A real boxer. And he had been a boxer all along.

"Woof!"

The End

About the Author

Stephanie Himango is an Emmy® Award-winning TV writer and producer with a love for boxing, boxer dogs and self-development studies. She is a senior producer and writer on a television program about innovation, and she has covered every Olympic Games from 2004 to 2016. For more than a decade, Stephanie immersed herself in broadcast journalism through her work in network news, and the stories she covered included the September 11th attacks, natural disasters, high profile court trials, drug cartels, the economy, health, pop culture and stories about people making a positive difference in the world. Prior, Stephanie studied Chinese and lived in Hong Kong for six years where she completed a Master's degree, wrote for an interior design magazine and earned a black belt in Goju-Ryu style karate. Stephanie's exposure to elite level athletes, creative entrepreneurs and people of many cultures has informed and inspired her quest for life-long learning.

Contact: getintheringbruno@gmail.com.

Also by Stephanie Himango

Stephanie Himango published her first non-fiction book *Another Door Opens* in 2014. *Another Door Opens* began as a creative storytelling and photography project documenting doors and the stories of people who live and work behind them. Originally posted on Stephanie's *Another Door Opens* blog, the 10 short stories in this book are the first 10 stories on the journey of the *Another Door Opens* project. Everyone has a story, and by sharing these stories, Stephanie hopes to inform and inspire, to open doors, and in turn, open minds. *Another Door Opens* is available on Amazon.

Made in the USA
Coppell, TX
20 November 2019